ALLEN RIDER GUIDES

RIDING: BUYING YOUR
FIRST HORSE

ALLEN RIDER GUIDES

Riding: Buying Your First Horse

Marilyn Ross-Kinister

J. A. Allen

London

British Library Cataloguing-in-Publication Data.
A catalogue record for this book is available from the
British Library.

ISBN 0.85131.625.5

© J.A. Allen & Co. Ltd., 1995

No part of this book may be reproduced, stored in a retrieval system, or transmitted, in any form or by any means, electronic, mechanical, photocopying, recording or otherwise, without the prior permission of the publisher. All rights reserved.

Published in Great Britain in 1995 by
J. A. Allen & Company Limited,
1 Lower Grosvenor Place, Buckingham Palace Road,
London, SW1W 0EL.

Typeset in Hong Kong by Setrite Typesetters Ltd.
Printed in Hong Kong by Dah Hua Printing Press Co. Ltd.

Cartoons by Marilyn Ross-Kinister
Designed by Nancy Lawrence

Contents

	Page
INTRODUCTION	7
1 MAKING THE DECISION TO BUY	9
Purchase Price	9
Methods of Keeping Your Horse	9
Full livery : Part livery : Working livery : Do-it-yourself livery (DIY)	
Other Considerations	12
2 WHAT TYPE OF HORSE?	14
Age	16
Young horses : Older horses	
Colour	17
Sex	18
Stallions : Geldings : Rigs (cryptorchids) : Mares	
Type	19
3 HOW TO LOCATE A HORSE	20
Magazines and Newspapers	20
Commonly used advertisement abbreviations	
Agencies	22
Agents	22
Auctions	22
Dealers	23
Riding Schools, Pony Clubs, etc.	24
Breed Societies	25

4 TEN QUESTIONS TO ASK BEFORE MAKING THE TRIP 26
   Is He as Described? 26
      Height : Age : Colour
   Is He Good in the Following Respects? 27
      Traffic : Box : Shoe : Clip : Catch : In the stable : In company
   Is He Suitable for My Needs? 29
   Is He Viceless? 29
      Crib-biting : Windsucking : Weaving : Rearing : Bolting
   Does He Have Any Veterinary Problems? 31
   Is He Fully Innoculated and Security Marked? 31
   Is He Straight in His Action and Unblemished? 32
   How Long Have You Had Him and Why Are You Selling? 32
   Does the Price Include Any Tack, Rugs or Equipment? 33
   What Facilities Do You Have for Trying the Horse? 33

5 TRYING THE HORSE FOR SUITABILITY 34

6 THE ETIQUETTE OF BUYING 40
   Advisors and 'Experts' 40
   Deposits 41
   Negotiations and Warranties 42
   Final Payment 45
   Insurance 45

7 THE VETTING PROCEDURE 46
   The Five Stages of the Vetting 48
      Stage 1 : Stage 2 : Stage 3 : Stage 4 : Stage 5

8 THE FIRST WEEK 51

   CONCLUSION 56

Introduction

This book has been written to help those of you who are considering buying your first horse avoid some of the possible pitfalls.

It will help you to decide *whether* to buy and *what* to buy, and guide you in simple terms through such aspects as vetting and warranties.

There are, however, two basic principles to remember. Firstly, there is no such thing as 'the perfect horse'. A more realistic aim is to buy an animal whose fault(s) you can live with. Secondly, the law, as it applies in the purchase of horses, is *caveat emptor* or 'let the buyer beware'!

1
Making the Decision to Buy

The decision to buy a horse can prove costly, both in terms of initial purchase and upkeep.

Purchase Price

This is dependent on many factors, including breeding, type, abilities and even the time of year. As with any other form of purchase the laws of supply and demand directly affect the price. Therefore, as winter approaches and the animals become more costly to keep — and the thought of getting up at 5:30 a.m. to muck out and defrost frozen taps becomes daunting to the present owners — more horses will be offered for sale at a lower price. Likewise, as spring approaches and thoughts turn towards sunny days and horse shows, prices will rise.

As any dealer will tell you, however, they can always sell a good horse, regardless of the time of year. Horses with ability will always bring a good price. Realistically, for a first horse of average conformation, well schooled and able to compete at Riding Club level, I would expect to pay between £1,800 and £2,500. Do be prepared to compromise on price. Ultimately, a horse is valued in terms of what he is worth to you; if he is perfect for your purposes, it is worth paying a little bit extra for him!

Methods of Keeping Your Horse

The cost of upkeep can vary enormously, depending on the

area, the method employed and the facilities available. If keeping your horse at a large establishment, your bill may be subject to VAT and this must be taken into account when considering your budget.

FULL LIVERY Full livery means that the stable staff undertake to do everything concerned with the wellbeing of the horse, including feeding, grooming and exercising. Because this is an all-inclusive service, charges can be as high as £75 a week.

This would seem to be the perfect method for the busy horse owner with limited time, but it does mean that you miss out on a lot of the pleasure of 'doing' the horse yourself.

If you do choose this method, make sure that you fully understand what services are included in the charges, and which are additional. Worming, shoeing, plaiting and clipping or using the indoor facilities may all incur extra costs.

Obtain a receipt, not only for your weekly/monthly payment, but also for any tack or equipment that you leave for use on your horse, and make sure you have a written contract agreeing terms and conditions. It is also important to establish what action may be taken in your absence should your horse become ill or sustain injury.

Worming, shoeing, plaiting and clipping may all incur extra costs.

— *Making the Decision to Buy* —

PART LIVERY With part livery the stable staff undertake to carry out certain aspects of the work involved and the owner does the rest. They may well, for instance, give the morning feed, change rugs and turn the horse into the field and leave the grooming, mucking out and exercising to you.

Costs will vary, dependent upon the services carried out, but will be substantially cheaper than full livery. Another advantage of this method is that it necessitates only one visit per day to the stables by you, saving time and fuel expense.

As with full livery, make sure both parties understand what is expected from the other.

WORKING LIVERY Working livery is not to be confused with part livery. This method is occasionally offered by riding schools and is an arrangement whereby the cost of the upkeep to the owner is lessened by the school having the use of the horse for clients at certain times.

The biggest drawback to this option is that the busy times of the school may well coincide with your leisure time — not to mention the detrimental effect of several different riders on your horse's schooling.

Do make sure that your horse will be available to you when you want him!

DO-IT-YOURSELF LIVERY (DIY) DIY is probably the cheapest option. With this method you pay for the stable and associated grazing and do all the work involved yourself. Rents may vary from area to area, as may the quality of buildings, quantity and quality of grazing and safety of fencing. As with everything, it pays to shop around.

Many DIY yards insist that you buy feedstuffs, hay and straw from them; take this into account — you may well end up paying superior prices for inferior goods!

Check that the established methods of management on the yard are acceptable to you. For example, some yards forbid the use of shavings as bedding which is of no use to you if your horse has an allergy to straw. Some yards restrict grazing times. Most establishments will insist on a regular worming programme for all the horses in residence, but this is not unreasonable because it protects everyone's interests.

Other Considerations

Regardless of where you are going to keep your horse at livery, it is important that your tack, equipment and feedstuffs are kept securely.

Many people prefer to have a small, secure area adjoining their stable, which they can keep locked. Obviously this is a good method for the individual owner because only they can gain access. However, the drawback is that, in the event of fire, for example, no one can rescue your belongings.

If a communal tack room is the alternative, my preference is for the door to be fitted with an electronic key pad device, the combination of which is made known to all the owners and which is changed at regular intervals when liveries leave the yard. This allows access to all authorised people, negates the need for keys which can be lost or forgotten, and ensures access when stable staff cannot be present. The key pad can be used in conjunction with a burglar alarm, which is activated when the door closes, and remains so until the key pad combination is used again.

Can your family cope if you are ill?

— *Making the Decision to Buy* —

Although it is possible to manage by keeping tack etc. at home, it does become wearing, items can be mislaid or forgotten, and it can make an awful mess of your vehicle.

Canvass the other members of your family. If you are ill, or need to go away, can they cope with the needs of your horse? If not, talk to the people at your livery yard, they may help each other in times of illness.

Make sure that in addition to the horse's keep you will have sufficient funds available for other outlays: shoeing every six weeks, annual innoculations and insurance as well as the inevitable vet's fees and repair and renewal of equipment.

Consider how much time you have available for your horse after your commitments at work and at home. If you will be restricted to riding only at weekends it may be more sensible and enjoyable to ride at the local riding school. There you would get to ride different horses, they would be made ready for your arrival and put away as you depart, there would be no mucking out, no tack cleaning and none of the inevitable sleepless nights that all horse owners endure at some point, but it is not as much fun!

Although it is not necessary to be an expert stable manager to become a first time horse owner, you must be realistic. Consult your riding instructor and horsy friends about your abilities and ask them to be honest about your level of competence. Many evening and adult education centres now conduct courses in stable management, and the British Horse Society offers an examination in competence for the non-professional horse owner.

2
What Type of Horse?

The type of horse that you *can* have may not be the type that you *would* have if your resources were unlimited, but various factors must have a bearing on your ultimate choice.

Your own age and physique – height and weight – must obviously be taken into consideration as well as previous experience and present ability. Ideally your height and weight should be in proportion to the horse, at least initially whilst you gain confidence. I would recommend that, if faced with a choice, it is better for the first-time horse owner to be under-horsed rather than over-horsed, within reason. Remember, a horse's ability to carry weight is determined not by his height but by his bone. The amount of bone is determined by encircling the cannon bone immediately below the knee with a tape measure and reading off the measurement in inches. A cob type of 15 hh is up to more weight than a larger horse with less bone.

One major factor has to be how you feel when on board. Normally, the sole of the rider's boot is level with the lower edge of the horse's belly. If it is lower than this, there may be some difficulty with the application of the leg aids but if the horse has a substantial barrel and the rider feels balanced then this should not be a problem. If, however, the horse is too narrow, the rider may experience a falling outward sensation when riding turns and circles, similar to sitting astride a gate which is being pushed to and fro. In this case the rider will never feel adequately balanced, a problem which could be accentuated when riding with a shortened stirrup for jumping.

— *What Type Of Horse* —

Ideally your height and weight should be in proportion to the horse.

It is important that the horse has a good front, i.e. a pronounced wither and a neck which is not too short and which has an upward arch. This enhances the feel of having plenty of horse in front of you, and gives confidence to the rider when carrying out downward transitions (changes of speed from faster speeds to slower ones).

The size of children's ponies can create problems if they are required to compete, because some classes are divided not only by the height of the pony, but also the age of the child rider. This means that only a child of appropriate age may compete on a pony of a certain size at many shows. At local level the schedule may be less rigid, but these restrictions should be borne in mind by those buying for a competitive child, or by a lightweight adult considering the purchase of a sturdy pony for themselves. Conversely, a competitive adult may have to buy a horse which is technically too big if competing at the higher levels; the stature of the horse must be in keeping with the demands of such competitions. A slight lady rider, for example, may appear to be over-horsed, but, if riding at this level, the rider's experience should be commensurate with the job in hand.

— *Buying Your First Horse* —

It is vital that the horse you buy is suited to your present needs. Possibly, after 12 months ownership, you will feel that you have outgrown him in terms of experience rather than size. That will be the time to sell him on and replace him with a more capable animal. It is kinder in these circumstances to let him go to a new home where his abilities will be appreciated, rather than try to make him keep pace with your ambitions. When you sell, be prepared to lose a little on the price you paid for him. He is, after all, a year older and you have had much fun and tuition from him, and that is worth any loss you will incur.

Age

Most first-time buyers want a horse of between six and 10 years old, when a horse is supposed to be in his prime. This demand is likely to be reflected in both the price and availability of these animals. However, the two opposite ends of the spectrum are worthy of some consideration, especially to those with limited funds.

YOUNG HORSES Youngsters of four and five years old tend to be dismissed by first-time buyers as likely to be problematic owing to their youth and lack of experience. In fact, a young horse who has been properly broken and schooled could prove to be a better buy than an older horse which has had time to learn bad habits. If the trainer's job has been done correctly, the young horse should have a good attitude to his work, and this, coupled with a calm temperament, would make him a better investment than a wily ten-year-old. Also, buying at this age gives much more scope for education and achievement for both horse and rider, and could well do away with the necessity to part company after a short time; hopefully his experience and ability will increase in ratio to your own.

OLDER HORSES More mature horses should not be discounted either. A horse of 11 or 12 years of age still has many years of useful and active life ahead of him. Many top competition horses are still winning in their late teens. What he lacks in terms of youth will be outweighed by experience, and provided that he has been well looked after, the years will weigh lightly on him.

The older horse can be an excellent schoolmaster for a nervous rider being less likely to seek out weak spots in the rider's confidence and ability than a younger horse. Small signs of mileage may be apparent in his conformation — deepening recesses above the eyes, a slight dip to the back, small lumps and bumps on the legs — but small defects like these should not affect his soundness, and he would be considerably cheaper to buy than a younger animal.

A word of warning is in order when considering the purchase of an older horse. It is remarkably difficult to tell the age of a horse after the age of eight. It is imperative that, unless the horse is known to you or has registration documents of some kind, you have his age approximated by a vet.

Colour

Inevitably, people will have personal preferences when it comes to colour. I consider colour to be relatively unimportant when making the decision to buy, except in the case of older, grey horses who have a tendency towards the growth of melanomas (skin tumours). However, many people do have a particular colour in mind and their determination to purchase a horse of that colour can blind them to any faults that an animal may have in temperament, conformation, or even suitability!

On the other hand, there are many misleading ideas with regard to colour. For instance the old adage:

> One white sock, buy a horse
> Two white socks, try a horse
> Three white socks, look well about him
> Four white socks, do without him!

Some of my best horses have had four white socks!

Chestnut mares are considered notorious for being temperamental, hence the number of advertisements declaring 'not mareish' when these animals are concerned.

Black horses are always popular but in my experience are more susceptible to sarcoids (angleberries) than others.

Coloured horses, i.e. piebald and skewbald, which were once shunned as being 'common', are now increasing in popularity, and much sought after.

Grey horses are hard to keep clean, especially when kept out, and in common with all horses with pale skin and pink noses can suffer from a form of equine sunburn on their noses in the summer.

On balance, it is fair to say that a horse should be purchased on his merits with colour and associated minor drawbacks being only a secondary consideration.

Sex

Personal preference will also play a part when choosing the sex of your horse.

STALLIONS Uncastrated male horses are unsuitable purchases for the novice horse owner. Although some stallions do have an equable temperament they can be difficult to handle, especially at certain times of the year, and their management is best left to the more experienced.

From a practical point of view, it can be difficult to find livery accommodation for stallions. They have special needs such as reinforced boxes, door grilles and well-fenced separate turnout areas. They can exert an upsetting influence on the other horses present (and their owners!) and can, at worst, prove dangerous.

GELDINGS Castrated male horses are more amenable than stallions and are generally a good prospect for the novice owner. Many livery stables will still graze mares and geldings separately because even geldings may fight over a harem of mares and risk injuring themselves. However, in terms of riding and handling, geldings usually prove reliable.

RIGS (CRYPTORCHIDS) Rigs are unsuccessfully castrated male horses. These horses can be extremely dangerous because their temperament can change quickly from quiet to lethal, either when being handled or out in the field. A 'gelding' who shows signs of aggressive or violent behaviour − particularly if he starts to round up mares if grazed with them, carrying his head close to the ground − should be blood tested for cryptorchidism.

MARES The advantage of a mare is that, should something render her useless for riding, you could still breed from her. It must be remembered, however, that breeding from a mare whose conformation and soundness are questionable is both foolish and costly, and the decision to breed is a great responsibility.

In addition, the facilities required for in-foal mares and those with a foal at foot are not usually available at the average livery yard, consequently this needs serious consideration together with the extra financial burden and the owner's possible lack of experience. Should you still feel that you would like to breed from your mare, bear in mind that it will be at least three years before you can even sit on the offspring!

It is also a fact that some mares can become difficult when they are in season, and during this time may not be their usual trustworthy selves.

The dilemma of a horse's useful working life being brought to a premature end through illness or accident does not just apply to the owners of mares, and it is for this reason that I strongly recommend you take up the 'Loss of Use' option on your insurance policy.

Type

Necessity, rather than preference, will play a part when it comes to choosing the type of horse. You must take into account the manner in which you are going to keep him. A cob type for example, would probably be happy to live outdoors all year round, as long as he is given sufficient food, clothing and natural shelter. This would not appeal to a less robust animal, nor would it be fair to keep him under such circumstances. Methods of keeping are dealt with in Chapter 1 but this must be a key issue in a decision on type.

3
How to Locate a Horse

Magazines and Newspapers

Certain equestrian periodicals carry advertisements for horses and ponies offered for sale, as might the classified columns of your local newspaper. Bear in mind that many of these advertisements will have been placed by private vendors, and as such are not covered by the Sale of Goods Act, so you have fewer rights should a dispute arise. You need to show that you exercised reasonable caution when making the purchase in the first place.

Beware of several advertisements placed for different animals under the same contact telephone number. This could well be a family giving up horses or a riding school decreasing its stock, but it could also be a trader giving the impression of being a private vendor. This practice is illegal, traders are required to state their occupation in their advertisements.

Horses bought privately should still be as advertised, although approximations of height and age are common. Determining the exact height of a horse is a complex and time-consuming business requiring removal of the horse's shoes, a totally level standing surface, and a particular position of the horse's head. Many vets will, when examining the horse for purchase, simply put 'aged' on the certificate if the animal is over eight years old, for fear of litigation. It is hardly surprising, therefore, that the private vendor does not want to commit themselves to these details!

— How to Locate a Horse —

When reading through advertisements try to glean what is not said, as well as to interpret what is. If only 'good to catch, box and clip' is stated, it may mean that the horse is difficult to shoe for instance, or not good in traffic. Therefore, ensure that you query these points when viewing the animal. Always take someone with you who can verify the answers given by the vendors in response to your questions, and request a full written description from the vendors.

COMMONLY USED ADVERTISEMENT ABBREVIATIONS

hh	Hands high
PC	Pony Club
RC	Riding Club
ODE	One day event
SJ	Showjumping
HT	Horse Trials
XC	Cross Country
PtP	Point to Points
PN	Pre Novice
LR	Leading Rein
FR	First Ridden
WH (P)	Working Hunter (pony)
SH (P)	Show Hunter (pony)
MW	Middleweight
HW	Heavyweight
M&M	Mountain and Moorland
PBA	Part-bred Arab
NF	New Forest
TB	Thoroughbred
TBX	Thoroughbred cross
(R) ID	(Registered) Irish Draught
LHC	Life Height Certificate
BHS	British Horse Society
BSJA	British Show Jumping Association
HIS	National Light Horse Breeding Society (HIS)
WB	Warmblood

Agencies

In recent years a new concept of horse purchase has flourished, that of the computer-based agency. Vendors register horses for sale with the agency, and pay an agreed fee for this information to be circulated to interested parties.

As a potential purchaser contacting the agency, you would be questioned about the type of horse you are seeking, the price you want to pay, and the distance you are prepared to travel to view. Details of horses that meet your requirements will then be forwarded to you, possibly with a video showing the horse in action. This service is available to buyers at a nominal cost, or, in some cases, free. Advertisements for these agencies can be found in the classified columns of many horsy-interest magazines.

Agents

An individual acting as an agent may simply, as above, pass on details of animals for sale and contact telephone numbers. However, some agents actually house the horses and use their own facilities in order to trade. Either their name, the fact that they are an agent, or that the horse is 'for sale on behalf of a client' should appear in their advertisement.

If the animal that you purchase proves to be unsuitable, a contact agency cannot reasonably be held responsible. They simply passed on details that they believed to be correct. If, however, the agent entered negotiations on the owners behalf, they could both be deemed liable, but proving this may well be very difficult.

Auctions

Auctions take place regularly throughout the length and breadth of the country. Normally, two types of sale are held, warranted and unwarranted. At an auction, you may have fewer rights than if, for instance, you bought from a trader. Read the conditions of sale carefully; they are normally printed in the catalogue, but may also take the form of a notice on the wall near

— *How to Locate a Horse* —

the auctioneer's box. These conditions will cover not only such subjects as deposits and payments, but also what is covered by the warranty. It may come as a surprise to discover that the warranty at some sales does not cover sex, height, age or colour, but does include soundness of wind, limb and eye, and being quiet to ride. Make sure that you find out what length of warranty is applicable, and listen carefully to announcements as the horse enters the ring in case the warranty is withdrawn at the last minute.

At some sales a vet is in attendance and will make basic checks on a horse's soundness, but if you buy a warranted animal you can, and should, get your own vet to examine him when you get him home. Ask the vet to run a blood test in case the horse has had substances administered to keep him sound for the duration of the warranty period, which is usually 48 hours. You must notify the auctioneers of any untoward findings and return the horse to the point of sale.

Two important points to remember:
1) If you buy any horse outside the ring it is deemed to be unwarranted.
2) Bear in mind that, at auction, bids are still made in guineas. This can make a substantial difference to the price if you are still thinking in pounds. Take this into account when making your bid.

If you do decide to buy at auction make several visits as a spectator before you go to bid and try to familiarize yourself with the proceedings. Mistakes can prove costly.

Dealers

Dealers' advertisements can be found in most equestrian magazines, or under the heading 'Horse Breeders and Dealers' in *Yellow Pages* and other directories. A better method, in my opinion, is by word of mouth. Speaking to horsy people in your area will probably bring the names of local reputable dealers to light. Satisfied customers are a business person's best advertisement.

— *Buying Your First Horse* —

Try going along to a few local horse shows. Many dealers use these as a showcase for the animals they have for sale, as do many serious competitors who need to sell the occasional young horse to subsidize their interest in the sport.

Having located a dealer, contact him and explain the type of animal you are looking for and the price bracket. Arrange to go along and see anything in his yard that may be suitable. One advantage is that there may well be several horses to view, saving you time and expense. The trial facilities are likely to be better than average so that the horses can be shown to the best of their abilities.

When you arrive, take stock of the overall appearance and feel of the place. The horses should be well stabled and bedded, with clean coats and be in good condition. Staff should be cheerful, helpful and knowledgeable and the tack should be clean, of good quality and in good repair. Beware of dingy stables bedded with a handful of straw, thin horses with unkempt manes and tails, and sullen staff who enter stables with lighted cigarettes.

Many dealers have regular equine residents on their yards. These familiar old hands who, having served as a schoolmaster, return every so often in part exchange for a faster model, are perfect for first time buyers. Their price can be very reasonable too.

Remember that when you make a transaction with a trader you have substantially more legal rights than when purchasing from a private vendor.

Riding Schools, Pony Clubs, etc.

As a general rule I would advise against buying horses that have been used in a riding school. They may have become set in their ways according to school routine, may not move forward from the aids after being 'deadened' to them by numerous mixed ability riders, and may take exception to leaving the other horses after being used primarily as a member of a ride.

However, a visit to the local riding school, or to a Riding Club or Pony Club rally, can prove very useful for horse seekers. Ask the instructors and other owners present if they know of a

— *How to Locate a Horse* —

They may take exception to leaving other horses.

horse that is for sale. The chances are, if they do know of one, they will also have a good knowledge of the animal's character, abilities and behaviour and the reason for the sale. If you are lucky, the horse in question might even be present and you will be able to speak directly to the owners.

Breed Societies

If you have a preference for a particular breed, try contacting the appropriate breed society. They can be helpful in locating animals for sale, and can offer invaluable back-up advice to first-time owners.

4

Ten Questions to Ask Before Making the Trip

You can save yourself time, expense and frustration by asking a few pertinent questions on the telephone before making the trip to view a potential purchase.

Is He as Described?

It is a rare event indeed to view a horse which is exactly as you imagined him to be on reading the advertisement. You will have your own interpretation of the phrases describing the animal, and the owner's opinion of the horse will be coloured by his familiarity with him.

HEIGHT This is one of the major bones of contention. Horses are measured in hands — a hand being four inches. In my experience most advertisements err in respect of the animal being smaller than stated. When scrutinizing the 'Horses for Sale' columns in search of a 15.2 hh, it may well be worthwhile telephoning about a 16.2 hh to ascertain whether that is in fact the actual height as opposed to the approximated height.

AGE Normally the age is checked by looking at the horse's teeth. However, this is a difficult science, even for the practiced, so it is worth asking whether the present owners can verify the horse to be the age stated. Registration papers from a breed society will show a date of birth, or there may be a veterinary certificate from a previous examination available.

— *Ten Questions to Ask* —

COLOUR This is another subject open to interpretation. Palomino — which should be a golden colour with a white mane and tail — can vary from pale cream to chestnut! However, unless you have your heart set on a specific colour, this is not a major drawback.

Is He Good in the Following Respects?

TRAFFIC This is important unless the horse is being bought specifically for competition use. In this country it is almost always necessary to ride along a stretch of highway to reach bridleways or riding areas. This can be a nightmare with a traffic-shy horse, making you a danger to yourself and other road users. Bear in mind though, that horses are living, breathing creatures, and no horse can be taken to be *totally* trustworthy in all traffic situations. Try to find out what he will and will not accept such as tractors, double-deck buses, motorcycles and heavy goods vehicles, and relate this to the situations that you will have to ride in.

Find out whether he will load into a horsebox or trailer.

— *Buying Your First Horse* —

BOX Find out whether he will load into a horsebox or trailer easily and travel well. Preparing your horse for a show and then not being able to persuade him to go in the horsebox is extremely upsetting. Although this is a problem that can be overcome, it is not really a problem the first-time horse owner wants to have to cope with because it can detract enormously from the pleasure you will get from your horse. Difficult loaders can make you very unpopular if you have to share transport to events with others.

SHOE Farriers are skilled craftsmen, having qualified after years of training, and good ones are sought after. Most are quite happy to deal with young horses' first experiences of shoeing, and quietly and patiently persevere until their young charges are *au fait* with the procedure. Frankly, they do not need to put themselves at risk with difficult horses, nor is it fair to expect them to do so. A horse that is difficult to shoe means that you will need to battle with him, on average, every six weeks, and if you are inexperienced at restraining determined horses it is a battle you will almost always lose.

Some horses will accept cold shoeing, but not hot shoeing. With cold shoeing, the burning on process which ensures a good fit, but creates acrid smelling smoke to which some horses take exception, does not occur. Although hot shoeing is preferable, providing the horse will stand quietly to be shod and has good feet, cold shoeing is an acceptable alternative.

CLIP Clipping is the removal of all or part of the winter coat to allow the horse to work without sweating and therefore losing condition. This is not necessary if the horse is doing minimal amounts of work, but will need to be done if you want him to be kept fit.

Even horses which are reasonably amenable to the clipping procedure may have ticklish places. You can get around this by using a different type of clip which leaves those areas untouched, or, in very difficult cases the vet can tranquilize the horse to enable you to cope.

Try to place what the owners tell you in the context of what you will need to do, and decide how much of a problem clipping will be.

— *Ten Questions to Ask* —

CATCH My own philosophy is that the two most frustrating things in life are a car that will not start and a horse that will not be caught in the field. It always happens when you need them most and there is nothing more infuriating than walking up and down the field as your horse gallops gaily to and fro, making you feel a total fool. Again, the problem is not insurmountable, but do you really need this experience?

IN THE STABLE A horse which is difficult to handle in the stable is not a worthwhile proposition for the first-time owner. Working safely in the stable is of paramount importance for the novice owner who does not have the experience needed to deal with flashing teeth and hooves. Remember, having a horse is supposed to be fun, owning a vicious horse could make you dread the thought of going to the stables.

IN COMPANY Ask whether the horse 'hots up', i.e. becomes excited when ridden in the company of other horses. A horse that can be ridden out quietly alone may become totally unruly when accompanied by other horses, or when taken to a show. With a horse such as this you could, at best, find yourself ordered off the showground and, at worst, find yourself in the local casualty department!

Is He Suitable for My Needs?

Be honest with the vendors about your experience and what you want to do. Give them the opportunity to tell you a potted history of the horse's time with them, their achievements with him and the type of work for which he has been used.

Is He Viceless?

Basically, a vice can be described as a habit which may have a detrimental effect on the horse's physical or mental wellbeing. Most of these are acquired by boredom or bad management, but certain stable vices can be picked up by horses kept in view of an affected animal. The law requires that such vices be declared at the time of sale.

— *Buying Your First Horse* —

CRIB-BITING The horse takes hold of an object between the upper and lower teeth — usually the upper edge of the stable door or a fence post in the field — and, arching his neck, draws in lungsful of air. This can cause weight loss and colic, and habitual cribbers show signs of unlevel wear on their teeth. This is known in the trade as 'laying hold of the door'.

WINDSUCKING Windsucking is the same vice as crib-biting except that the horse draws in air without holding on to anything with the teeth.

Both crib-biting and windsucking can be alleviated by using a strap which, when fastened around the horse's neck, prevents the arching of the neck to draw in air. Determined animals can get round the use of this strap by stretching the neck outward to suck in the air, giving the impression of the animal having hiccups.

WEAVING The horse stands with his head over the stable door, moving his weight from one foreleg to the other, swaying from side to side. The swaying becomes worse when the horse is excited at feed times, or when other horses leave the yard, for example. Replacing the top stable door with weaving bars or grilles can help, but habitual weavers may simply move back into the box and weave inside.

One of the major drawbacks of owning a horse with a stable vice is finding accommodation for him. Most livery stable and riding school owners are loathe to stable these horses for fear of reprisals from other owners whose animals may pick up these habits. Young horses, particularly, are likely to mimic these problems.

REARING The horse rears by lifting his front legs off the ground and standing on his hind legs. This is extremely dangerous because there is always the chance that he may lose his balance and topple over on top of his rider. This vice usually stems from the horse resisting the rider's forward driving aids, and these animals should only be ridden by experienced persons who can feel the loss of impulsion — forward drive — and send the horse forward strongly. A horse who has reared once will always rear again and is totally unsuitable for the first time buyer.

BOLTING Bolting can be a truly terrifying experience; the horse careers away with his rider, totally out of control. Confirmed bolters run away whenever allowed to travel at speed. Any horse, however, can run off as a result of fear — a car suddenly backfiring for example — and this is something that all riders run the risk of experiencing when taking up riding. One such experience should not label that horse a confirmed bolter.

Does He Have Any Veterinary Problems?

Problems such as a dust allergy or sweet itch, which are not life threatening but do require extra time, effort and finance may make this horse unsuitable. Make a mental note of what you have been told in response to this question and if you are not familiar with the problem ask a knowledgeable friend or look it up in a veterinary handbook. Consider what effect this could have on how you intend to keep the animal and whether it is something you could live with.

As a general rule I would not consider any horse which was receiving long term medication or anti-inflammatory drugs.

Is He Fully Innoculated and Security Marked?

Most horse owners consider it a necessity to have their animals vaccinated against tetanus and equine influenza. In fact, the production of an up-to-date vaccination certificate is now a requirement for entry at a number of shows and horsy events. If the animal is not innoculated, make sure that you allow for the cost of this in your budget if you choose to buy him.

Security marking is a definite advantage and is something which has grown in popularity recently, reflecting the growth in the number of horse thefts. Various schemes are available, some more visible than others, but the theory of recording the details of the horse on a central register and distributing these details to appropriate parties in the event of theft is basically the same.

In the case of both innoculation and security certificates, each time ownership of the horse is transferred the certificate will be amended to this effect, therefore this is an easy way to determine length and legality of ownership.

Is He Straight In His Action and Unblemished?

The answer to this question is pertinent if you have showing classes in mind for your competition interests because faulty action and the existence of blemishes will be marked down by the judge. However, for basic hacking and Riding Club activities small defects in the horse's movement are unlikely to have any adverse effects. In severe cases there may be strain on joints and ligaments, or contusions from one limb striking against another, but as this constitutes part of the vetting procedure any abnormality and its consequences could be discussed then. It would be highly unusual for a horse not to be considered suitable for general purposes on the strength of his action.

How Long Have You Had Him and Why Are You Selling?

Length of ownership can be checked with vaccination and security certificates if available, or if the horse has competed seriously he may have a checkable record with the governing body of that particular discipline.

Reasons for the sale must be plausible, such as his being outgrown or the owner going to university. 'Lost interest' may mean they tired of being bucked off!

— *Ten Questions to Ask* —

Does the Price Include Any Tack, Rugs or Equipment?

All items of equipment can prove costly when added to the price of the horse. It may well be possible to negotiate with the current owner for the purchase of these items but make sure they are in good condition. Not only will they be cheaper than new items, but you should have the added advantage of knowing that they fit, and that the horse is familiar with their use.

What Facilities Do You Have For Trying the Horse?

The facilities must be in keeping with what you will need to do to determine the horse's suitability for your purposes. Indoor or outdoor schools, an open field, some coloured and natural fences and a busy road are ideal but unfortunately rarely available. It is useless, however, to purchase a horse for any purpose on the strength of riding it along a dirt track. If reasonable facilities are not available, do not make the trip.

5
Trying the Horse for Suitability

After your initial enquiries about the horse, you will make an appointment to try him. Whatever time you agree with the vendor *do show up* and *be on time*. A lot of time and energy can be expended on making the horse ready for potential purchasers, and it is soul destroying if they do not show up. If, after making the appointment, you reflect on what was said and decide that the horse is not really what you were looking for, at least have the courtesy to ring the vendors and say so.

Make sure that you take clear directions to ensure that you will be punctual. Arriving before or after the time in order to 'catch them out' is futile. It serves only to antagonise the legitimate vendor, and there is no way the unscrupulous would fall into such a simple trap.

When you arrive, exchange pleasantries and ask to see the horse in his own box. Beware of the horse which is tied outside the stable, or one which is already tacked up. Look over the stable door and decide whether or not you like him. Although first impressions can be deceiving, if you dislike the colour, type or just the look of him, it is highly unlikely that you will ever cement a partnership.

Watch for signs of poor temperament, such as showing the whites of the eyes, ears laid back, or a swishing tail. Even if — as the owners will no doubt tell you — he does not carry out his threat to bite or kick, this horse could make you dread going into the box with him. Most horses with this type of character play havoc with an inexperienced owner's nerves, and soon gain the upper hand.

— Trying the Horse for Suitability —

Look around the stable for tell-tale marks on doors, walls or mangers for evidence of any of the vices outlined in the previous chapter. Is the hay in the net or rack wet? Is he bedded on shavings rather than straw? Both these facts could indicate a dust allergy, which in turn may affect his breathing. Has he coughed whilst you have been watching? Check his rate of breathing by watching the rise and fall of his flanks. On average the breathing rate is 12 per minute but slightly above or below this is acceptable. However, if it takes a double effort of the flanks to help expel the air, the horse probably has broken-wind (Chronic Obstructive Pulmonary Disease — COPD) and is therefore unsuitable for purchase.

Take note of the horse's overall condition. He should be well covered with flesh, have a shiny coat and bright alert eyes. The stable should be light and airy with plenty of good quality bedding.

Horses in poor condition are sometimes offered for sale, usually with a suitably plausible sob story. Do not be taken in and buy this horse out of misplaced sympathy. In some cases there may be a true and rational explanation for his condition, illness for example, but I would not recommend purchase.

Putting weight on a horse which was previously undernourished requires expertise and if done without due care can cause serious problems. Also, consider the costs incurred returning these horses to their proper state. It would be better to spend that money on the purchase of something already in good order.

Do not allow yourself to fall prey to anthropomorphism, i.e. attributing human traits to animals. You may think that if you feed him and lavish care upon him, he will reward you with undying love and affection. This may well happen but in some cases he will grow, become strong and quickly realize his superior strength. It may well be that he was underfed to dampen his volatile temperament and out of the best of intentions you might have created a monster.

Assuming that you are happy with what you have seen so far, enter the box. Assess his conformation if you can, or at least run your hands down his legs and feel for any lumps and bumps that you cannot identify. It really is not necessary for

— *Buying Your First Horse* —

you to have a wealth of knowledge in this respect, this is what you are paying the vet for when he performs his inspection. This also applies to ageing the horse and assessing his movement. A basic understanding gleaned from your previous experience, perhaps from your lessons at the local riding school, should stand you in good stead.

Ask to see the horse's feet picked out, and then handle all four feet yourself. Look for any deviance from the normal type of hunter shoe, and signs of unlevel wear. If anything appears unusual, ask the reasons why.

See the horse led out of the box wearing a headcollar, not a bridle. Cob types can become headstrong when being led and you need to see if this applies to this particular animal. Look for sweat marks that may mean he was ridden prior to your arrival to quieten him.

Watch him being led away from you in a straight line, turned to the right and led back. A horse should always be turned to the right when being led because this allows him to describe a wider turn which places less demand on his balance. Turning right also ensures a safer clearance for the handler's feet and, more importantly in this case, gives the observer a clear view.

Ask for this process to be repeated in trot. Make sure that he starts and finishes the trot within your vision. Starting and stopping put more strain on the legs and he may show lameness at these points. His head carriage should remain steady throughout, and the handler should not hold the lead rein so tight that it restricts free movement. Any 'bobbing' of the horse's head signifies lameness, and if in doubt you should not attempt to ride him. Nor should you attempt to ride him if he gives you the impression at this stage that he could prove to be too excitable for your experience.

If you are still happy with the horse, ask to see him tacked up. Watch this taking place, and make a mental note of any tack that you are not familiar with, such as tongue grids, brush prickers and Kineton nosebands. Gadgets are always there for a purpose, and you must query what that purpose is before you mount!

Now is the time to see the horse ridden. Does he stand still

— *Trying the Horse for Suitability* —

whilst mounted? This may seem a small consideration but it is infuriating and potentially dangerous to be hopping about on one leg attempting to mount as the horse keeps dancing away. I also have a theory that if the horse has no respect for your wishes when you are unmounted, he will certainly not have any respect for them when you are on board.

Initially, see the horse ridden in an enclosed space, such as an indoor or outdoor school. Does he go quietly and calmly in walk, trot and canter, turn and circle smoothly and have effective brakes? Watch for any signs of napping — refusing to go forward — near the gate, or other signs of resentment of the aids, such as bucking when asked to canter.

If you wish to see him jump, ask to see him approach in both trot and canter, over coloured and natural obstacles. Does he approach calmly, without rushing? Does he attempt to refuse or run out? Consider his shape over the fence; he should make a clean arc (bascule) and land quietly, moving forward and straight away from the fence. He should not land, buck and turn all at the same time!

The final stage of this part of your assessment is to determine whether the horse can, and will, rein back. Do bear in mind that this is a fairly advanced movement and that a young horse may well not have achieved this level of training. In the case of an older horse it is not an unreasonable request. When reining back, the horse should remain attentive to the aids, stepping back cleanly with diagonal pairs of legs, lifting them clear of the ground, whilst remaining in a straight line. He should not throw his head in the air, stiffen his back and drag his feet. Many horses will behave perfectly up to this point, but when asked to step backwards will actually stand up on their hind legs.

If satisfied with his work in an enclosed arena, ask to see him ridden in an open field, both in the slower gaits and in gallop. You may well see a totally different character emerge, but if he stays sane and sensible it is time to return to the enclosed area and ride him yourself.

When you have mounted, does he stand still whilst you adjust stirrup leathers and girth? Do you feel comfortable with his height and width? Begin by walking round quietly to familiarize yourself with him, and let him adapt to the change of rider. Do not go any faster until you have checked the brakes by asking him to halt, stand still, and walk on again. Proceed into trot. Does he follow your instructions quietly and obediently? When you feel confident, try a canter. He should take the correct leg and maintain the gait easily. If he feels lazy, this does not necessarily make him unsuitable; it is easier to sharpen up a lazy horse than to calm an overzealous one. Ride towards and away from the gate. Sensing a change of rider may cause him to try you out and resist. If he does, at least you will know whether you can deal with any awkward traits. Now ask yourself, 'Did I find him a pleasure to ride?'

Jump only if you are capable of doing so. You will have seen and assessed the horse's ability over fences with his usual rider, and it is very difficult to ride to the best of your ability on a strange horse, in a strange place, with an audience. Even a good horse will refuse with a nervous rider, and you owe it to the vendors not to spoil their horse's way of going because of your misplaced pride.

Now try him on the road. Ideally, as before, see someone else on him first. If he appears to be unperturbed by his surroundings, mount and try him yourself. I like to take the horse out on a short hack, with another horse for company initially, and then separate from his companion and return home alone. This helps to check not only his behaviour in traffic both accompanied and unaccompanied, but also his behaviour with other horses. It also tests his willingness to leave other horses and remain obedient to your wishes.

On your return, do not go straight into the yard but ride past the entrance before allowing him to turn. Does he become difficult when asked to pass the gate, or rush back when allowed to head for home? All horses will 'hang' a little for home, but some become virtually unmanageable and are therefore unsuitable for the inexperienced.

Following these stages when trying a horse will help you satisfy yourself that the horse is suitable for your needs and whether you would be comfortable and confident with him. However, it is impossible to cover every possibility because all

— Trying the Horse for Suitability —

horses — like people — have personal idiosyncracies, but these should endear and not endanger.

Most vendors will agree to your returning for a further trial, the danger being that someone else may come along in the interim. Most good horses get snapped up very quickly, and it is unreasonable to expect a vendor to hold the horse from sale until you return. However, it is better to be safe than sorry, and there will always be another horse.

If you are satisfied with the horse, it is usually necessary to leave a deposit with the vendor, subject to a successful vetting. The nature of deposits and other financial matters are discussed in Chapter 6.

6
The Etiquette of Buying

Advisors and 'Experts'

Most vendors are happy for a potential purchaser to bring along a more experienced person to view the horse. It is best for your advisor to accompany you on the first visit, and not waste everyone's time by making two trips.

Your advisor should know your level of experience and ability, the method by which it is intended to keep the horse and be able to ride and assess the horse's suitability for your purpose. With this in mind, their experience – hopefully practical and built up over a number of years – will stand you in good stead. They will be able to discern the relevant factors and dismiss the side issues. For example, a horse offered for sale as 'not 100 per cent in heavy traffic' may be a suitable (and cheap) purchase if you only intend to use him for hacking over the moors, and your advisor should recognise this.

One of my pet phrases is 'Bring me a vet but not an "expert"'. Vets will view a horse in terms of his physical ability to perform the function required of him. Occasionally, they may have cause to mention any quirks of temperament that they discovered, a child's pony that kicked or bit during the inspection, for example, but their view is usually fair and objective. Not so the self-professed 'experts'. These are the people who, after spending 12 months mucking out at the local riding school and leading ponies about, put themselves forward as suitable companions for horse buying trips, and make a charge for doing so. In my experience many such people think that their role is to denigrate the horse so that it might be bought more cheaply. In truth they may well cause the purchaser to pass over a suitable animal. It always saddens me when purchasers miss a good horse on the advice of an 'expert'. Beware of the 'expert' who is looking for a horse to suit themselves, rather than one to suit you.

Whoever you take to view the horse, be totally sure of their integrity. It is not unheard of for some of these people to approach the vendor privately and offer to swing the deal for some financial reward. If the vendor is a responsible person, no such 'understanding' would be entertained. Nonetheless, some people can earn quite a nice living by this method, and recommend the purchase of an unsuitable animal to line their own pockets. Any horse that is genuine will sell on his own merits.

Having decided that a particular horse is suitable, you will now enter a sensitive period of negotiation and unwritten rules.

Deposits

You must expect to leave a deposit, usually subject to a satisfactory vetting. The amount of deposit is open to discussion between you and the vendor, but normally £100 would be reasonable. Obtain a receipt, and make sure that it states whether the deposit is returnable and under what circumstances. For example, if the horse fails to meet the vetting standard for your purpose, the deposit will be returned. If you simply change your mind and decide not to buy — especially if you take a week to do it — the vendor is perfectly entitled to keep your money. Other potential purchasers may well have been lost through your actions, and the vendor will have to go through the whole advertising process again at further expense. Those persons then reading the advertisement may well recognize the description of the animal or the telephone number and assume that, because it remains unsold, the horse is not genuine. This explains the frequent appearance of advertisements in the equestrian press saying 're-advertised due to timewasters'.

A cash deposit is usual, in view of the time which elapses between a cheque being issued and clearing the bank, for the reasons outlined earlier in this section.

Having paid your deposit, contact your vet immediately to book him for the horse's examination. Your receipt may well say 'subject to vetting within a reasonable time', which to most people means a week to ten days. If after this time I had received no word from the purchasers about the vetting, I would re-advertise the horse, and notify the purchasers of my actions.

Negotiations and Warranties

Do not assume that, because the horse is advertised at a particular price, the vendor will accept less; this is a common fallacy. If you like the horse, he is worth paying for. It would be more sensible to negotiate for the price to include items of tack, equipment or delivery. The time to enter into these negotiations is on your first viewing visit and no later.

Many dealers can relate stories of people enquiring about a horse and going through a lengthy viewing process and then admitting that they only have, for example, £500 less than the asking price to spend. A patient dealer could probably produce something else within your price bracket, a less patient person,

Something more in your price bracket.

— The Etiquette of Buying —

especially a private vendor, would probably throw you out. If you cannot pay the full price, make this quite clear to the vendor when making your initial telephone call. They can then decide whether they are prepared to negotiate to that extent. Do not waste the vendor's time.

Some of your negotiations may include a warranty agreement. This may take two forms:

1) The vendor may write 'quiet to ride in company or alone, good to box, shoe, clip and in traffic and free from vice' on your receipt. This is a form of guarantee that the horse is as stated.
2) A professional vendor may well offer to exchange the horse if he proves to be unsuitable. This agreement relies on a suitable replacement being available of course, and it is reasonable to expect to have to wait until another horse is available. There is always the risk that the horse offered in exchange may not be — in your eyes — of the same value as the one you have. This problem has to be looked at objectively.

Horses do come under the 'Sale of Goods' Act of 1979, and should be suited to the purpose for which they are intended. Unfortunately, this does not take into account the other factor on horse performance and action — the rider.

If you buy a horse, ride it badly and manage it inadequately, things will go wrong. The value of that horse will be substantially reduced, and this will have to be taken into account in the exchange.

Beware, however, the unscrupulous vendor, who will allow you to buy a horse knowing he will prove to be more than you can handle to ensure that you will be back to exchange him, usually for one of a much lesser value. Once in this downward spiral, it is very difficult to get out except at great financial loss.

Most professional vendors will tell you if the horse you want is going to be suitable or not. The genuine dealers want you to be happy with your purchase, and have an interest in the horse's wellbeing. The professional vendor has a reputation to uphold, and has many years' experience — listen to his advice.

— Buying Your First Horse —

Many people will not listen to sound advice because of their inflated egos, so if all else fails the vendor will probably write something on the receipt that makes his feelings known and to protect himself and his interests. For example, the receipt may say 'sold as unsuitable' or 'sold to your advisor's approval'. If this happens to you, and the horse does prove unsuitable for you, swallow your pride and go back. A good dealer will be only too happy to help you put matters to rights and sell you something better suited to your abilities. Whatever the reason, if you are unhappy with your purchase you must give the vendor a chance to put it right. Nothing will be gained from publicly criticizing this person without speaking to them about the problem.

Having read all this you may be contemplating asking to have the horse for a trial period. Personally, I would not allow a horse off the yard on such an arrangement because within a week he could, subjected to mismanagement, be a totally different animal.

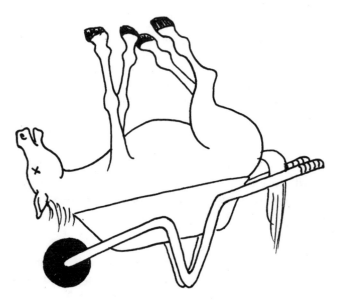

Insure the horse before you collect it.

― The Etiquette of Buying ―

Final Payment

So, you have negotiated and agreed the price, the horse has been successfully vetted, and now you have to pay up! Do not expect to pay by cheque and take possession of the animal all on one day. The cheque will have to clear before the horse can be expected to leave the yard. Obviously, this does not apply to cash or bank draft transactions.

Insurance

A word of warning: INSURE THE HORSE BEFORE YOU COLLECT IT. Make sure that the insurance covers any injury sustained whilst in transit. Although it is a remote possibility that something may happen, you must protect your investment.

7
The Vetting Procedure

Having found your horse, negotiated the price and left a deposit, you will now need to organize a veterinary examination of soundness and suitability for purchase.

There has been much debate about the viability of these examinations, with certain horses failing with one vet and passing with another. It is true that many horses who have, at some time, failed a vetting, have gone on to many years' active service without any adverse effects. There are also many experienced horse people who are capable of establishing soundness in a horse, but they cannot be expected to detect problems in the heart or eye.

My advice is that it is better for the first time buyer to engage the services of a vet and to be guided by his experience and advice. Ask horsy friends and acquaintances for the names of vets whose practices are involved with plenty of equestrian work; it helps if you have faith in the vet's judgement. Bear in mind that you are paying for his professional opinion, you do not necessarily have to take it!

When you first contact the vet you will need to supply certain information, so have this to hand:

1) Your name and address and, possibly, telephone number.
2) The name, address and telephone number of the vendor. He may well contact them direct to arrange a mutually convenient time.
3) The place where the vetting is to take place, and directions if necessary.
4) A brief description of the horse he is to examine.

The Vetting Procedure

5) The type of work that you are purchasing the animal for. Do be specific about this because it will form the basis of the examination. A horse which would pass the examination for Riding Club activities may well not pass for three-day-eventing!
6) Whether or not you will be present at the examination. I recommend that you be there if at all possible. The vet can then explain his findings to you, and this will give you a greater understanding of any defects or injuries that may come to light.
7) Your riding ability and experience. This will help the vet's assessment of suitability in terms of the horse's temperament.
8) The asking price. But, under no circumstances should the vet enter into negotiations on behalf of the purchaser.
9) Finally, if you have noticed anything about the horse, such as a nasal discharge, or some scarring, now is the time to mention it, so that he can give attention to it.

Unless otherwise specified, the horse will undergo a full vetting procedure. Partial vettings are available which cover only specified aspects, e.g. eyes and heart, as are insurance vettings, which are a modified and less stringent version of the full procedure.

The price of a full vetting can vary enormously but between £100 and £180 appears to be a reasonable average for a local vetting where the vet does not incur too many travelling costs.

Although some full vettings include the taking of a blood sample as standard practice, many do not, and if you request this an additional charge will be made. One part of the sample is left with the vendor and the other remains in the possession of the vet. Should the horse become lame within two weeks of purchase, the vet's sample will be sent to the laboratory for analysis to ascertain whether any anti-inflammatory drugs were present when the sample was taken. These substances would disguise signs of lameness in the animal at the time of examination. The sample left with the vendor enables him to have his own analysis done.

X-rays do not constitute part of the full vetting, but many veterinary practices now have mobile X-ray machines and these

X-rays do not constitute part of the vetting.

can be used to good effect if there is reasonable cause to fear early signs of disease in a limb or foot.

A full vetting normally consists of five stages and takes approximately one and a half hours. Prior to examination, the horse must be left in the box and not exercised. He should be clean, but his hooves should not be oiled because this could disguise defects.

The Five Stages of the Vetting

STAGE 1   The first stage of the procedure takes place in the box. Initially the vet may observe the horse over the stable door, not only to see if there are any signs of stable vices but also to assess the way he stands. Resting a hind leg is common, and probably means nothing, but the resting or pointing of a foreleg would immediately be suspect. The vet will then enter the box, and proceed to check the horse's pulse, respiration and heart, verify the age, and check the eyes with an opthalmoscope whilst out of the harsh daylight. If any serious problem surfaces at this point, such as a heart murmur, it is possible that the vet will recommend ending the examination.

STAGE 2   The horse is brought out of the box and undergoes a nose to tail check including examination of all four legs for

— The Vetting Procedure —

any enlargements. He will then be walked and trotted in hand to assess his action and soundness. Some vets may carry out a flexion test on each limb in turn. This simply entails holding the leg up for a short time, with each of the joints bent, before asking the horse to trot away immediately the leg is replaced on the ground. The extra strain placed on the joints may make the horse trot away lame. It is up to the vet to interpret the result of the test, and what effect it would have on the horse's soundness for your purposes.

STAGE 3 If the horse is broken, the third stage is carried out under saddle. Some vets may ride the horse themselves but more usually the vendor rides. The purpose is to see the horse worked fairly vigorously to check for any defects of wind, heart or limb. The horse will be trotted and then cantered around the vet, and close enough to him for any noises in the breathing to be heard. Finally, if facilities allow, the horse will be galloped. Immediately after working, the heart will be examined again.

If the horse is unbroken, this exercise can be carried out on the lunge.

Obviously, the level of the horse's fitness must be taken into account during this stage. He should be exerted — not exhausted.

STAGE 4 After exercise, the horse is returned to the box and allowed to recover for up to 30 minutes. This constitutes the fourth stage of the vetting. Certain types of lameness only show up after the horse has exercised and then rested, and we need to know that he recovers normally from activity.

STAGE 5 Finally, the horse will leave the box again for a further examination of his heart rate and soundness in action. This, as in the second stage, is carried out in hand. If all is well he will be given a certificate of soundness. This certificate must be filled in by the vet and contains details of the tests, a full description of the animal concerned, date and place of the examination, and the names and addresses of purchaser and vendor. It will also list any minor defects which, in the vet's opinion, will not affect the horse's usefulness for your purposes.

This certificate only applies to the horse's soundness on that day, and does not render the vet liable for injuries or disease which become apparent at a later date.

The outline of the vetting procedure in this chapter is given only as a very general guideline as to what to expect. Certain tests may be added, substituted or omitted. Rest assured that the vet will carry out any tests he feels necessary to convince himself of the horse's soundness.

8
The First Week

Prior to your new horse arriving, you have much to do. You will need to prepare a stable, preferably steam cleaning it with disinfectant to ensure total cleanliness. It is likely that you will be required to keep your new horse in an isolation box, separate from the other horses on the livery yard, to prevent cross infection should he be harbouring any ailments. Isolation can last up to two weeks.

A good, deep bed should be made ready with adequate banking around the edges of the box to protect his fetlock joints from injury should he dash around excitedly when he arrives. If there is an automatic drinking bowl check that it is fully operational and is well scrubbed out.

If you have bought new tack, it is very important that the leather has been well oiled and made supple prior to use.

It may be useful to contact your chosen vet to check that he can accept you as a client, and give the farrier plenty of notice of the time that your horse will require shoeing to ensure that he can fit you in.

Ask the previous owners for all the helpful information they can give you such as:
1) Date he was last wormed, what product was used, and whether he has an adverse reaction to any veterinary product.
2) All relevant documentation — security marking, tetanus and flu vaccination certificates, and any breed society registrations, with dates for appropriate renewals.
3) A feeding routine — times, feedstuffs, amounts and any additives. Try to adhere to this if possible, but if you must

— *Buying Your First Horse* —

change, make all adjustments SLOWLY.
4) Date his teeth were last attended to. Horses upper teeth grow downwards and outwards, and their lower teeth grow upwards and inwards, so their chewing action causes wear that leaves a chisel-like edge on the surface. Therefore, at least once a year but preferably twice, the horse's teeth need to be checked by the vet or a specialist horse dentist, and the surface rasped level once more. This is a minor procedure and not costly but if unattended can cause all sorts of problems such as head tossing, resisting the rein aids, and being difficult to bridle.
5) Find out what rugs he wears, if any.

When the horse arrives, take some photographs of him from different angles clearly showing any markings. Make a detailed written description of him, taking special note of any scars or marks that would differentiate him from another horse of similar height and colour. Take more photographs through the changing seasons so that, should he ever go missing, you have detailed descriptions of him, regardless of the time of year.

Take photographs of him from different angles.

— The First Week —

It is important to establish a routine quickly because this will help him settle in more easily. All horses vary but any initial nervousness caused by his change in environment can be overcome by calmness on your part. Do not be disturbed by the fact that he looks a totally different character from the horse you remember buying because it can take up to two weeks for them to settle in. Because of this, it is important that you establish your seniority in the partnership straight away. Do not give too many titbits hoping to make friends, he may well take this as an invitation to begin to nip!

Always put on his headcollar and rope and tie him to a ring in the wall to muck out and groom. Make sure that he will move over when told and stands quietly whilst you work.

I lead unknown horses using a lungeing rein rather than a lead rope for the first few days. I find that the extra length affords greater control should the horse become excitable or difficult.

Many horses will try it on in their new home and you must deal with this in a positive way but not be cruel and frighten him. Firm but gentle is the right attitude.

If he is not allowed into the field until the quarantine period is over, boredom may cause him to become naughty. Make sure that he has at least two exercise periods a day in these circumstances and, if you can, lead him out in hand to pick at some grass. Some horses like to play with stable toys such as an old tyre or football suspended by rope from the ceiling, or a tastier alternative such as a turnip or swede.

If he does become boisterous he may try to dash out of the stable door as you try to lead him out. This is very dangerous because you could be crushed between horse and door, or he may injure himself on the jambs. Always maintain a good hold on the bridle or headcollar, and make sure that he stays straight and well under control both entering and leaving the box.

Do be consistent with any reprimands. Do not correct him one day for a wrongdoing and ignore it the next. To do this creates confusion in his mind. Is it naughty to do that or not?

When the time comes for him to be turned out, put on his headcollar but do not clip the lead rope onto it. Rather, thread the rope through the back of the headcollar noseband, holding the two ends in your hand. With this method, should he get excited and charge away, you can simply let go of one end of the lead rope and pull it through, releasing the horse with headcollar still intact. This will only apply if the horse is very excitable; if he stays reasonably sane it is acceptable to attach the lead rope in the usual way. Before releasing any horse into the field, turn him to face the gate whilst you unclip the rope, this ensures that you can reach safety should he decide to kick out.

As a general rule I do not recommend that horses be turned out with headcollars on in case they get entangled in something. However, I do leave a headcollar on a new horse for a few turnouts in case he proves difficult to catch.

If possible, avoid turning your new horse directly into a field full of others. Ideally, put him into an adjacent field, preferably one with post and rail fencing, so that they can become aquainted at a distance. Post and rail fencing, as opposed to barbed wire, helps prevent injury if a conflict occurs close to it. After two or three days they should be reasonably tolerant of each other and prepared to share the same field, although some fighting is inevitable to establish the pecking order. Make sure that you stay close by, ready to rush to the rescue if things get violent! ALWAYS remember to check your horse thoroughly for signs of injury after bringing him in from the field, even when he has settled in.

When you go to catch him the first time, hide the lead rope in your pocket or under your coat, approach from the direction of his shoulder and speak quietly to him, proffering a titbit. Take hold of the headcollar noseband gently and attach the lead rope. It may well be that after two weeks isolation, he is not eager to return to his box. You must perservere and catch him, and not leave him in the field. Enlist some help if necessary and get him in somehow! He must not profit from being naughty. He may be unwilling to be caught for a few days until he gains confidence in you, and you must be patient.

When you begin to ride him, stay in the indoor or outdoor school until you are confident of each other. Any nervousness on your part will be transferred 'from the brain down the rein' and convey itself to him. For this reason, have someone

— The First Week —

accompany you for your first ride out. If you go alone in trepidation, he may well sense your fear, begin to spook at imaginary objects and become nappy.

If things do begin to go wrong, seek the advice of a more experienced person as to the possible causes; you could, inadvertantly, be making some mistake. This person may be able to sort the problem out for you, or explain how to overcome it. If it is something more serious, contact the previous owners, explain what is happening, and give them the chance to sort it out or give some advice.

Inevitably, after taking possession of the horse you will have doubts and worries about having done the right thing. This is known by the very scientific name of cognitive disonance, and it happens to everyone! Believe me, it *will* pass.

Conclusion

I hope that this book will help give both purchasers and vendors a greater insight into each other's needs but, more so, I hope that it goes a little way to protect the interests of the most vulnerable party in all these transactions: our silent friend — the horse.